Horns

Tiffany Midge

Winner of the Wilder Series Poetry Book Prize

Two Sylvias Press

Two Sylvias Press
PO Box 1524
Kingston, WA 98346
twosylviaspress@gmail.com

Cover Photo: Charley Flyte
Cover Design: Kelli Russell Agodon
Book Design: Annette Spaulding-Convy

Created with the belief that *great writing is good for the world*, Two Sylvias Press mixes modern technology, classic style, and literary intellect with an eco-friendly heart. We draw our inspiration from the poetic literary talent of Sylvia Plath and the editorial business sense of Sylvia Beach. We are an independent press dedicated to publishing the exceptional voices of writers.

For more information about Two Sylvias Press please visit:
www.twosylviaspress.com

First Edition. Created in the United States of America.

ISBN 978-1-948767-21-7

Praise for *Horns*

Tiffany Midge's *Horns* is a comedic romp and a razor-edged burlesque, with seriousness in its bones. Midge's cast of characters, drawn from pop culture, history, and literature in equal measure, is epic, from the Maiden on the Land O'Lakes Butter Box to Martha Stewart to Corpse Bride, the Girl Scouts of America to Satan himself. Her structures are as abundant as her performers. There are lists, outlines, contemporary ghazals and sonnets, interviews, statistical round-ups, and marriage vows. There's nuance, too, and spot-on moments of lyricism: "Her dresses, hung in the closet like sides of beef," she writes in one poem. And at the end of "Matrimonial Vows for Cannibals:" "I will savor your brain for last, that soft, sweet rind, / your edible, desirable, loveable mind." True to its title, *Horns* is sharp, dangerous, and melodic, a collection that resonates with joyous critique. **—Diane Seuss**, author of *frank: sonnets*

℃

I often read books without any idea what I'm hungry for. Turns out *Horns* has the mysterious ingredient. Like the star of Midge's poem, "Voracious Insatia," I am *she* who "wants those words... wants those liturgies, those witnesses, those gospels," who "combs those truths through her hair like honey rinse..." Yes, I want all that, and these poems deliver. This collection celebrates women as transgressive agents—*she-devils* with sharp horns made of wit, wielded to poke, prod, and stick it to the patriarchy. **—Rena Priest**, author of *Sublime Subliminal* and *Beaches*

℃

Tiffany Midge's "Horns" is the rare kind of book that delights, enrages, provokes, and invokes laughter all at once. From giving us the voices of monster's brides and zombies to interrogating "Indigenous Census Statistics," Tiffany's irreverent, always surprising poems practically beg to come to life as you read them. You may already know her for her humor essays, but reading her poetry, you can see a writer who can flex between worlds of horror and philosophy, satire, and political critique with equal power. A must-read from a voice that demands—and rewards—attention. Midge is a writer to remember. **—Jeannine Hall Gailey**, author of *Flare, Corona* and *Field Guide to the End of the World*

෴

In this lyric collection, Midge frankensteins hybrids, patches disparate fragments into forms that reflect the grotesque as a sort of caricature to mock power structures. She's by turns evocative, provocative, and funny as hell—like all good humorists, simultaneously hilarious and deadly serious, as she reimagines such Great American (Indian) Novels as *The Dreamcatcher in the Rye*, the use of *Savage* ____ in the titles of Native/White interracial romance novels whose lovers lack "commod bods," Satan's horned daughter struggling as the ultimate interracial child, or the Indian Princess gone MIA from the Land O' Lakes box: "O our butter maiden / brought all the boys to the yard /… / the only Indian woman gone missing / that anyone…cares about." **—Heidi Czerwiec**, author of *Fluid States*

Acknowledgments

The author gratefully acknowledges the magazines, journals, and anthologies where these poems, some in slightly different form, first appeared:

"Viewing the Pandemic Museum's Room of Masks: the Smithsonian, Washington, DC, in the Year 2051," Create Health campaign with Terrain and *The Black Lens*

"Washington's Monster Beats COVID," Public Intellectuals

"Distracted from COVID-19, Attention Shifts to MIA Maiden from Land O'Lakes Butter Box," Poets.org Poem a Day Series, November 2020 (Thanks to Heid Erdrich. And thanks to Billy Collins for selecting it to read on his web-blog)

"Re-Writing the Great American (Indian) Novel: Classics Edition," "Indigenous Erasure Poem," *Waxwing*

"Sheltering," *Massachusetts Review*

"The Down There Narratives," "Lipstick for Jesus," "The Corpse Bride Examines the Habitat of her Species," "Law and Order," *Yellow Medicine Review*

"Love's Ideal Envisioned by a Satyr," *Apex*

"Sixth Street Sonnet #1, #2, #3," *Okey-Pankey*

"Sex," and "Dream of the Fisherman's Wife," *South Dakota Review*

"Savage Ghazal," "An Evening Meal," *As/Us*

"Interview with the Carbon Gods," *Tattoos on Cedar: Washington Poet's Association Anthology*

"Winter," "*Memoirs of a Widowed Starlet* by Anne Darrow," *Stirring*

"Portrait of a Backwoods' Wife with an Axe to Grind," *North American Review*

"Amateur Psychoanalysis of Children's Literature," "Erotica Writing Workshop Imagined," *Queen Mob's Tea House*

"Miss Borden's Account of Things," *Weird Sisters: Lilac City Fairy Tales Vol. 3*

"Horns," reprinted in *Towers & Dungeons: Lilac City Fairy Tales Vol. IV*

"My Father's Mistress," *Shenandoah*

"The Monster's Bride Questions the Motives of Her Creator," reprinted in *A Face to Meet the Faces: An Anthology of Contemporary Persona Poetry* and *Best American Poetry Blog*, June, 2010, guest ed., Reb Livingston

"The Monster's Bride Questions the Motives of Her Creator," "Zombie Escape Route," "Divination Map for Lost Boys," "An Appeal to the Reckoner of Sand," "Love's Ideal Envisioned by a Satyr," "Miss Borden's Account of Things," and "Horns," *No Tell Motel*

"Monster Guide to Make Poem," *Mud City Review*

"Matrimonial Vows for Cannibals" appeared in the anthologies *America, What's My Name: The "Other" Poets Unfurl the Flag*, ed. Frank X Walker, and *Undead: A Poetry Anthology of Ghosts, Ghouls, and More*, eds. Bianca Lynne Spriggs and Katerina Stoykova

"The Girl with the Snake Tattoo," "Indigenous Census Statistics," *Hunger Mountain Review*

I am grateful for the support of my mentors, co-conspirators, and comrades who have contributed to this book and made poetry and literature possible. Special thanks to Charley Flyte (Mohawk and Oglala Lakota) for her beauteous cover photo.

Table of Contents

III.

Horns

For Ruth and her Coming of Age

There's a point, around the age of twenty, when you have to choose whether to be like everybody else the rest of your life, or to make a virtue of your peculiarities.

—Ursula K. Le Guin

Beware; for I am fearless, and therefore powerful.

—Mary Shelley

I.

The Monster's Bride Questions the Motives of Her Creator

The plugs jutting out from her neck:
she's curious, what are they for?

The fiery thoroughfare of crisscrossing scars
from temple to jaw, brow to ear:
should she look for something implicit there?

One eye brown, pilfered from an orange-haired
prostitute in Potter's Field; the other fixed askew
in her head, a child's like-new ornament:
is he a misogynist? Did his mother abandon him?

One arm, the muscular backhoe of a fieldworker's
connected to the jagged star of a hand:
she wonders, is she expected to work?

The vagina, intact and as pretty as postcard sunset:
should she ruin it for him?

The abdomen owns the legacy of multiple births,
a miller's wife spitting out babes like peas:
is there room to grow more?

What hair that's left is black as licorice,
sparse on her scalp like a locust-run crop:
does he secretly love his sister?

Her dresses, hung in the closet like sides of beef,
taffetas, crinolines, colors of esplanade sherbets:
should she dance for him?

At night, locked in her chambers,
she hears desire's low growl, smells iron, lust, rain:
what does it mean? Is it for her?

Law and Order

While it's illegal to throw snowballs in Belton, MO
and flying a kite is forbidden in Schaumburg, IL,
in the Midwest a pastor can publicly claim gay people
are possessed by fart demons that drive pigs to suicide.

In Oregon and New Jersey, it's illegal to pump your own gas.
In Kern County, CA, it's illegal to play Bingo while drunk.
But in New York, a woman who wins a three million dollar
lottery can get away with defecating on her boss' desk.

In Illinois, you can't hunt bullfrogs with a firearm.
In Tuscaloosa, FL, you can't give animals alcohol.
But in Seattle, WA, there's no law
against the Aquarium hosting a public Valentine's Day
octopus mating ritual—
there's no law against canceling it
for fear the rite might turn to cannibalism.

Did you know in Honolulu it's illegal to annoy a bird?
And in Arkansas there's a law against pronouncing
their state name as "Ar-Kansas?"

While you can't use a pogo stick on a city bus in Fairfax County, VA,
and a man with a mustache may not kiss a woman in Eureka, IL,
there's no law against marrying your red Chevy Corvette.

No law prohibiting crowdfunding for potato salad.
No law against drinking coffee from beans secreted by civet cats.
No law that restricts throwing a quinceañera for your poodle.
No law against painting graffiti on live snails.

Viewing the Pandemic Museum's Room of Masks: the Smithsonian, Washington, DC, in the Year 2051

Cy-Docent No.16-C guides our guests through a labyrinth
of suites and galleries, their voice resonant as a spoken word poem.
"Had there been conflict? Why yes, in the planning stages of the museum,
before ground was broken for its place, its own space, on the National
Mall."

A pause to survey an expanse of wall within the rotunda;
an installation of N-95 PPE appears. At first, the masks
seem to be apparitions, like holograms from a Disney
theme park. But then it's clear that they're actual—
that the masks are concealed within the wall,
that the masks *are* the wall. An optical illusion.

Each mask, perhaps thousands of them, lift off
from the achromatic wall taking flight like a kaleidoscope
of silver butterflies heading into the dome of the rotunda.
Visitors let out a collective gasp.

"Each mask has been fitted with a motorized set of wings
and its own power source. They will evacuate through the opened
dome and are programmed to collect in the cherry trees
on the museum grounds. But don't worry, the masks are organic-
friendly and will not harm any bird or living thing."

No.16-C pauses and continues, "The installation you just witnessed
is called *Transformations,* a kinetic assemblage in homage
to the perished and for their loved ones and survivors
during the 2019-2021 COVID Pandemic."
Several, if not most of the guests, recall those times,

some thirty years earlier, when the world was plunged into crisis.
And so many lives had been lost.

The last of the butterfly masks are seen fluttering through the top
of the dome. Blue sky and sunshine shimmers beyond.
Cy-Docent No.16-C shuttles the visitors to the opposite side
of the gallery where a Cy-Harpist plays a spirited interlude.
The guests take up the live wicks offered and alite the rows
upon rows of candles—a ruminative mood enshrines the chambers.
Cy-Docent No.16-C continues leading the guests down to the end
of the hall that leads to another ornate gallery.

Washington's Monster Cheats COVID-19

Deep within the laboratory, the mad doctors toil
reanimating the horror the village idiots delivered.
They stitch its bits like a jigsaw—
the sophomoric smirk, those extra tiny hands
and perverse pompadour.
They necromance its black heart
back to beating and pump its veins full
of the elixirs and potions that make
their stockholders smile. Then hose it down
and give it a fresh shellac,
prop it up like one of Madame Tussaud's,
a pig on a spit, or a spangled trick pony.
As predicted, the media with its pitchforks
and torches storm the castle gates,
while the monster tweets,
"AAAHG, YOU'RE FIRED, FIRED."

Monster Guide to Make Poem

Writing tip: Monster say narr-a-tive poem too *tell-y*.
Break up story-poem into image. Fracture.
Monster like *smash-y* poem. Not *tell-y* poem.

Monster write coyote poem. All coyote howl.
That what coyote do. But who care? Cliche. Monster
make them curse instead.

Bleep-bleepidy-bleep-bleep
all over lunar eclipse.
Monster no like well-thumbed
volume of shop-worn cliché.

Writing tip: Monster not like re-dun-dant.
Monster see "con-stant nagg-ing" in poem; Monster cry.

Monster re-create noun into verb: "Tinsels," and "Cottons"
to make image of snow. Monster feel proud. Monster like
nouns re-created as verbs. Monster big on re-creation.

Monster like taste, smells, touch, sound,
thing to see. Except fire. Monster not like fire.

Monster think poet should be specific, personal,
not general or abstract. Cryptic, esoteric story
not help Monster connect, Monster have no purchase
or investment in story only writer know. Bring story
into sharp relief, *spec-i-fic-i-ty* monster's friend.

Monster no like surreal image.
Make no sense. Like in Sesame Street song—

"one of these thing not like other,
one of these thing just not belong."

Writing tip: Monster no like flower poems.
Flower poem about flower too flowery, re-dun-dant.
Meta flower poem. But sometime flower
must be written about. Flower pushy like that.

Monster no have grasp of articles and con-junc-tions.
Sometime that okay. Monster no like Lat-i-nate words,
or pol-y-syll-a-bic words, Monster like one syll-a-ble noun
and verb. Monster favorite word cat.

Monster like best one syll-a-ble nouns with slant
or end rhyme. They make poem be-bop-py, monster
like sync-o-pa-tion. Monster like poem to dance.

Memoirs of a Widowed Starlet by Anne Darrow

The truth? they ask. The truth.
The truth is I wanted to pummel
my body against him like a sea wave
against a cliff. Every time I saw him it was
all I could do not to throw him down and ravish
him like a starved lioness. And it was not the ravishing
I craved, transparent as dragonfly wings, no, it was him, it
was who I was when in his presence, all that he inspired, that
intangible largess of desire. Especially when he murmured in my
ear—*you're the most virtuous woman I've ever known, I love you for
it*—I had to grip the edges of an imaginary railing and dig my nails into
my palms to keep from screaming my joy. Simians prefer blondes they say

but everyone knows even Marilyn dyed her hair.
When that last airplane tore him down and he fell
from his empire, the last vestige of my bleeding heart
plummeted those stories with him. *But did he love you?*
they ask. Can an Ape aspire? Dream? I hoped it to be so. I did,
but I never knew. The public wanted to believe he scaled the Empire
State Building out of blind, violent desire, but did he? Or was it the view?
He thought he was protecting me, of course, but in the end, he perished trying.

When we were new, he would bring me lilies.
        I'd be swept into the jungle scent of his arms,
        his teeth a forest of bamboo, his mouth a deep, dark Nile.

Amateur Psychoanalysis of Children's Literature

Oompa Loompas—representative of id, ego
and superego's integration.

Eat me, drink me, tell me again all the ways Alice
isn't acting out a Christ Complex?

Sure, Pippi Longstocking has Daddy issues,
but what's more concerning, have you seen her horse?

Though often misdiagnosed as a compulsive literalist,
when it comes to Amelia Bedelia's affliction there is no DSM-VI listing.

Does George suffer from a Cinderella or Oedipal Complex?
This is undecided, but clearly, his keeper is a giant banana.

Freud believed that spiders are the unconscious' symbol for vaginas—
what does that say about Wilbur (a pig) and Charlotte (a spider)?

Green Eggs and Ham is just another way of denying one's male
and female latent phase of development.

What James is actually doing with a sky-born peach remains to be seen
but plenty of people can see it's a giant piece of ass.

"Willy Wonka," is that not the most penis-ey name you've ever heard?
Each child is a different deadly sin.

Dick and Jane don't cotton to coincidence. Dog is God spelled backwards,
and Spot is Tops, writes Jane in her synchronicity diary.

It never was a dream, the lands Max embarks upon, the lands *Where the Wild Things Are,* but man's journey into his subconscious.

For Veruca Salt to be put right, like all narcissists of her ilk, requires no less but a good thrashing.

Goodnight Moon or as poet Dylan Thomas raged against the dying of the light, do not go gently: a bedtime story for the elderly.

The Very Hungry Caterpillar, not to be confused with *The Human Centipede.*

Everyone Poops—symbol of anal development phase or manifestation of castration anxiety?

Are You My Mother is the refrain in every therapist's office, in every lover's bed.

Attack of the Fifty-Foot Woman on Post-Its.

--After Beth Ann Fennelly

Harry just wants her money,
philandering bastard,

                but Nancy loves him,
                loves him still.

                                "Don't leave me Harry."

"We should have left
you in that sanitarium."

                Meanwhile, cut to the floozy
                back at the fleabag motel.

                                  "Something's happened
                                to Mrs. Archer!

Ahhrhrhhhhh!"

Eight hooks, four lengths of chain,
forty gallons of plasma
and an elephant syringe.

Overactive pituitary?
Some sort of radiation?

Tear gas, grenades.
"I can't shoot a lady!"

"Wadda ya want me to do,
salt her tail?"

"She finally got Harry
all to herself."

Zombie Escape Route

Zombie Escape Route sounds like an indie band
someone's nephew named Arturo plays bass guitar for.

It sounds like a speedy exit away from boorish hoards
who insist upon the multiplicity of ways to exhibit the following:

"I can't hear you over the sound of how awesome I am."
It sounds like a euphemism for getting out of a bad marriage or a dead-end
    job.

It might be the cocktail your bartender recommends
the night before you leave for prison.

Or what you'd drink the first night after getting out of prison.
My sister asked, "Why would you want the zombies to escape?"

Zombie Escape Route is the new crack.
I have at least five different writer-acquaintances using zombies

as their subject matter. Their thematic uses of zombies
is currently up for debate; there's the xenophobic angle;

the Americans as out of control consumers; or the fragile line
between humanity and barbarianism.

Zombies are the new black.
Pride and Prejudice has been revamped as *the* classic zombie love story

just when I thought *Night of the Living Dead* was.
Actually, I don't think there is a classic zombie love story. Yet.

ZER is the new MIA, and the new politically incorrect term for DNR.
Zombie Escape Route is the name of a convalescent home I'd want to retire to.

It's the name of Dick's Cheney's new yacht.
It's the name of a new candy bar I'd want to buy stock in.

Let's call Zombie Escape Route the new port of call for Princess Cruises.
Zombie Escape Route is the new Heaven, the new afterlife.

A new obstetrics term, Zombie Escape Route is what I'm calling my vagina
now.
It's my new group on facebook, twenty-seven members strong:

Organize Before they Rise. Our motto, don't get caught off-guard on Z-Day.
Go ahead and laugh but when you're surrounded, you'll have wished you
joined.

Zombie phenomena is a sociology class at Yale,
right up there with pirates and the vampire oeuvre.

What's stalking you down the halls of academia?
Zombies are the new fire.

Zombies are the neo-nouveau-nouveau, except there's nothing new about
them.
Who wouldn't want to be a zombie's kind of zombie?

The men's cologne, Axe, is being trademarked for zombie defense.
Zombie Escape Route is the title of my new poetry collection.

It's the new Campbell's Chicken Noodle Soup.
It's the new TV.

It's the new Duncan Hines Devil's Food Cake.
Zombies are the new vampires.

Zombies for Jesus.
Honk if you love zombies.

Zombie Jesus Day is the new Easter.
Zombie on board.

Beware of Zombie.
Go Zombie Green.

Zombie: A Love Story.
Sex, drugs, rock and roll, and zombies.

Have you hugged your zombie today?
Do you know where your zombie is?

The early zombie gets the worm.
A zombie in need is a zombie indeed.

You can lead a zombie to water but you can't make him drink.
A rolling zombie can gather no moss.

Don't count your zombies before they're hatched.
Don't look a gift zombie in the mouth.
All good zombies must come to an end.

Love's Ideal Envisioned by a Satyr

Her legs must be long as rockets, rubbery
as chicken bones soaked in vinegar.

She must be ethereal, hands like talons to stoke the tender coals
he gathers in the woods.

She must arrive on the tail of an exodus, an eviction, or banishment.

She must be Thumbelina-small, fit snug in the cup of a thimble.

She must reject him; this is imperative,
the sharper the wound the more ferocious his longing.

The air she omits must trap his soul like a fly in thick, yellow butter.

Her skin must burn in the sun, her kinfolk
fashioned like dough from the legacies of pillage or rape.

Her heart must cut glass.

She must flourish in the bodies of caves.

She must have wings that touch clouds, and speak the language of crows.

She must disappear like the mist over a mountain at dawn.

She must have no work to keep him, her only occupation
is drawing breath fanned by the circles he runs around her.

She must drink from the ruins of dead boughs.

She must aspire after the hollow in wait of a center.

She must evaporate like sugar kissing the tongue.
For this, he only thinks he'll surrender.

Matrimonial Vows for Cannibals

I will forsake all bodies. I relinquish
all other holy, fossilized, recipes of depravity,
the relics and the mummies,
the remains and the newly fattened.

For you, yes, for you.

No snacks, no dishes, no wishes, no rations.

I give up the sphincters, the iris, the corns.
I give up the pinkie nails, the harelip, the Charlie horse.
I give up the tear ducts, widow's peak, the sciatic.
I give up the Achilles, the gallbladder, and plantar warts.

It was the knuckles I loved best.
So hard to give up, Darling, but worth it for yours—
each with a scaly patch like broken plaster
and that knobby dome of glass,
cartilage poised beneath that dimpled gap.

In each hair follicle I recovered amplitudes, restored vision to the blind.
In each eyelid fold I drove men to kill.
In each clavicle I fought against the snouts of beasts.

Tell me again how you love me, *really, love me.*

I sharpen your bones into knives, carve you into spoons.
I pound out viscera like a kitchen mat on the first warm day in spring.
I iron out that stomach fat, those jibbly jowls and love handles.
I fiddle with your middle, wreak fist to nail, scoop your lovely liver.

It is your corpse I love best.
Your tawny hide and wee-wee piggy toes.
Your scrotum's wrinkles, your lip's pretty sneer.
Your useless skin-tags, your elbow's pucker.

Darling, I love the Holocaust of you, the cadaver of you.
I love the splatter of you, the crop dusting of you.
I love the horror you are beneath the skin.

I love the tail-bone gristle, the oily tallow of shins.
I love the tomato-thick of your plasma.
The sinewy muscle pulled like happy red taffy.
I love the violence and the porno of you.
I love the post-colonial imperialism of you.
You are my last supper.
You are my sacrificial offering.
You are my fecundity, my profanity, my soylent green—

and after I make a meal of your limbic spectacle,
and after I chew the heartiest of your rubbery artery,
and before I peel away your hamstring pelt,
I will savor your brain for last, that soft, sweet rind,
your edible, desirable, loveable mind.

Miss Borden's Account of Things

Only the wallpaper—yellow cabbage roses
      trimmed with larkspur—can say.

I was of course indisposed during the awful
      business, eating pears in the carriage house.

That's how it went over, twelve stern men,
      incomprehensible! A proper lady

of distinction born into a family of textiles
      and cotton—to think it!

Looking over the damage, I thought, how curious,
      such winsome blossoms—

the blood—dappled athwart Abby's eiderdown quilt.
      She'd scream if she saw it.

Fourteen blows (not forty) to Father in the sitting room,
      a spectacle, his head lolling about

on the fainting couch like a crushed melon.
      In the séance, Lady Odiah relieved my burdens,

my misgivings licked clean as a cat.
      But I knew the ghosts were talking, voices

whining like distant violins, compromising
      my agency, telling me what to do.

To have tipped back Father's bourbon,
      ten thimblefuls, a right antidote

for such rancor harbored in my throat,
        might have done the trick.

But instead, I took the tea—cheap and plain—
        because the Pekoe had been misplaced.

And I burned the dress, an indication
        of guilt they said and took a bath.

Instead, I should have bought a hat,
        or a sash of ribbon. Red.

In the evenings now, on our stately porch,
        I languish, I wait. While overhead

geese drag the clouds like bridal lace,
        unworn and ruined,

bedraggled debris. Such terrible,
        fatal flowers, a waste.

divination map for lost boys

1 :: the sofa cushions? never mind
       whatever change you find should have happened
       years ago
2 :: as for the wishing-well gods
       forgetaboutit—he's never going to fit
       in your pocket slick as a guitar pick
       tortoiseshell true
3 :: peter advised *second star to the right*
       and straight on till morning and I've a hunch
       that's where your lover went
4 :: but maybe is lost between a clutch
       of stars bordering ursa major or tinkerbell's spell
5 :: remember that girl who could divine
       the future from fish guts floating in a bowl?
       viscera pretty as a sunset or offal is awful?
6 :: have you considered boiling the head of a donkey?
       no, I guess it'd make an ass out of you and me
7 :: so much depends on flicks from a candle flame,
       freckles on skin, cigar ash or the splattering issued
       from a good sneeze
8 :: necromancy is of course the creepiest—
       keep a few corpses around and your future is set,
       but is he even worth it?
9 :: by mineral, by bone, by ouija (james merrill's
       the changing light of sandover was ghost-written
       by ouija), by fig leaves, dust
       or needles; even the angles of geese, pig bladders
       or random ravings of lunatics, my personal favorite
       I don't mind saying
10 :: chance encounters with animals are most popular among poets,
       particularly if they're Native American

11 :: who hasn't attended to the shouts of blackbirds
        or exposed one's soul to the whistling elk at Yellowstone?
12 :: I've received gifts of tarot cards and books
        on I Ching and once walked into a restaurant
        bathroom to find a woman reading another's
        palm when she could have just as easily read
        the splash of urine into the toilet. There's a name
        for that—urimancy, swirling water in a cup
13 :: by trees, by opening the dictionary, by patterns
        of bees, seek and you shall find, seeds in bird
        excrement, looking over one's shoulder,
        particulars of objects found on the road
14 :: it all has meaning, it all leads somewhere, fantastical
        or perverse—even cheese for chrissakes!
        even spindles and snail tracks
15 :: but darling you won't find him there
        I know I've tried
16 :: you won't find him in the cracks formed
        by the heat on a turtle's shell
        you won't find him in oracle bones
17 :: I've been there, I once saved toenail clippings
        and facial hair and made up a ritual
        involving purple juice and the burning of sage
18 :: a conjure map? sure, why not, go ahead, give it a shot
19 :: anything to hook or snatch, or snag—
        Tick, tock, tick, tock, so goes the crocodile
20 :: you won't find him in lost shoes or the mold
        on old bread, not eggs or teeth or the howling of dogs.
21 :: clouds seem transparent, an easy puzzle
        but beware disruption by jets
22 :: labiomancy? to foretell by lips? you could ask your bestie
23 :: anthomancy, the plucking of flowers
        he loves me, he loves me not. Seriously?

24 :: one in a million, stranger things have happened
            you've heard them all never say never, right?
25 :: remember that penny? god. the one with his birth date
            his lucky penny left on my kitchen counter
            glued it to my forearm and wore it like that
            for a month but did I ever find him?
            and that other one, I still have the gauze left over
            from when he gave blood, along with the black gloves
            stolen from his book bag
26 :: gone
27 :: still gone
28 :: lost
29 :: you've stumbled upon and happened upon
30 :: spider webs
31 :: squirrel poop
32 :: seashells
33 :: russian girls slept with mirrors under pillows
            to foretell the faces of future husbands
34 :: dice
35 :: onions
36 :: cups
37 :: mistletoe
28 :: oil
29 :: beans
30 :: interpreting laughter
31 :: interpreting stomach gas
32 :: who will be the new king?
33 :: wait for which horse neighs at sunrise
34 :: hate your mother?
35 :: visit a freudian to read your dreams
36 :: you could listen to what yolks tell you
            will he, or won't he? where the hell *is* he?
37 :: you could seek answers in the coiling
            and uncoiling of snakes if you can stand it

38 :: sooth-saying by rose petals, poems in books

39 :: *Keep it simple,* advised the stranger on the plane
    to Denver—she was a goofy new-ager
    who nitpicked me to death: *don't drink*
    diet soda; I can see the aspartame in your aura,
    said after three whiskeys, *I'm fifty!*
    Can you believe it? Just look at me!
    Keep it simple, Darling, you'll find him. I did.

The Confectioner's Defense

A trap of sugarplums
and peppermint,
her house attracts
small children, so?

Let it please the court
there are worst things
than treacle icing
and spiced gingerbread.

Let us pardon
gum drops and licorice—
sugar's not important here,
after all there's a splinter

of uncertain motives
to every witch, so beware.
Those who submit
to sweets, wayfarers

and lost urchins alike—
these *snared and summoned
meats*, clearly,
deserved their fates, no?

Martha Stewart Muses in the Kitchen
While Making Deviled Eggs

Don't you think that more hors d'oeuvres should be "deviled?"

If my morsels aren't a little bit demonic what's the point?

A cookbook for post-apocalyptic zombies.
Possible titles: *Bone Appetit. Eat, Prey, Limp.* Chapter One: Ghoulash.

Tapenade is possessed by all the gargoyle sprites. Legion swine.

Smoked salmon canapes will make me turn my head all the way around.

I'd writhe for goose pate.

Lift my skirt and toss my panties to sailors for a mouthful of caviar.

Give me meringue divinity; extract the sore orange eye from the egg.

Fault the vulnerable souls.
Those urchins without boundaries.
My larder is dark-sided.

Dream of the Fisherman's Wife

—after the erotic woodcut of the ukiyo-e genre
by the Japanese artist Hokusai (1820)

Lover, to taste and not devour,
to breathe and not inhabit the breath.

Heaven, your arms python-resolute,
salt-fierce as any titan.

Open, close, clutch, cleave. I sing praise
for water, tide a veil caught in my hair.

Patrons, you must know
this is no dream.

You slide green as an eel
through the fabric of my nights—

your course needle-agile, quick and sharp,
a slick shawl beyond aspect and ratio.

Oh, Emperor! What oysters are these!
Before you existed only acts, mere pretending.

Even the moon is jealous.
She pouts despite her grand theater of stars.

My desire is an origami riot,
chrysanthemum melancholy.

My husband mocks me as an octopus' trifle.
You think I'm nonplussed? No, unimpressed.

He thinks me a garnish.
Lover, to you I am a radish.

A ravishing. A lavish
lasciviousness, a slavish thing.

Portrait of a Backwoods' Wife with an Axe to Grind

Tree. Babe. Last night's supper, a rabbit
stew I'd set traps for all month, an acre of corn I shucked

for a week, and he spoke just two words: *Tree. Babe —*
over and over like a parrot.

Sure was a whole other story through courtship,
ain't it always, though? You'd think men of grand myth,

those larger-than-life folk, could deliver
romance in proportion to the campfire ballads. You'd think

heroic, right? *Epic!* Wrong. How many hours did I pore
over the recipes; *101 Ways to Cook Mammoth.*

*How to Stretch a Carcass into Next Week. EZ Budgets
for Folk Deities.* When I begged for a holiday,

he said, *tree,* which means Eureka on business or Mount
Shasta again, a summit meeting on Redwoods, like that's a vacation.

So I says to him, *you love trees so much you should have married one.*
And he picks up his axe, heads for the door, eyeing me

all suspicious, like I'm gonna go Lizzy Borden
on him, and says, *Babe…* Just that, *Babe.*

The Corpse Bride Examines the Habitat of Her Species

It's too much to say *egg,* when there's so much
implied: pomegranate seeds, salmon
roe, clusters of purple grapes. She shrinks

to imagine it, those eggs, her own, aligned
in perfect rows within the cupboard of her womb
waiting for a reason to crack open. To declare

flower as benign, a hothouse exertion
of the heart, means something more: a hand
embracing a petal, an impotent bloom,

an early frost, something missing. Even
the bedding accuses her—
the crisp white sheets, flung like unfilled

crepes, especially the quilt nailed to a wall
assuming a status, a position, its attachment
to something solid. In the tub, water is contrary

to intimacy, its volume is only another body
of separation. She theorizes the nature of rooms
without windows; considers the sharp edges

of sunlight, the angles of precise planes
in accordance to latitudes of wind—
Where is that breeze coming from?

She charts the coordinates for falling,
the hazards of stairs, the invisible
structures of love, elusive as whispers.

Most noted is the absence of insects—
moths attracted to lamps, spiders in distress,
not even an ant scouting the kitchen

at the crest of summer; it's as if even the bugs
find such habitat unacceptable, unworthy
of expedition. Is this place really so inhospitable?

Her designs quite so dour?
Even the rug possesses an anchor,
even the wallpaper, despite its garish

appearance, is paired with clutching ivy—
all those painted flowers, in vibrancy
and spirit, reaching madly for the ceiling.

An Appeal to the Reckoner of Sand

—Archimedes set out to determine the number
of grains of sand that fit into the universe

Dear Archimedes, there is so much to consider when
every grain of sand is a possible universe unto itself.

Think of all the little gods who fall asleep at the wheel,
think of the hazards of creatures who forget to pray.

Think of worlds abandoning their factories of gold
for a more promising afterlife. Are they mis-guided, do you wonder?

Think of all the others who will stay—
so many micro-kingdoms armored with pearls and bones.

Archimedes, there are a thousand ways to listen to the rain.
Just as there are a thousand ways to count your grains of sand.

Tell me where the music of the rain travels after twilight?
Tell me the stories of beach glass, stars and water.

Einstein said only two things are infinite:
the universe and human stupidity, and he wasn't sure about the former.

Aristotle distinguished between the actual and the potential,
while Plato had two infinities—

the great and the small. Archimedes, where do you stand?
And the heart? Where is the heart in all of this?

Shakespeare wrote of infinite love, abstract yet true as salt.
You must have some explanation.

In a parallel world lay a parallel world. In a particle lay a particle.
Within matter, matter. At sixteen, my first love

gave me a gift just a week before drowning. His gift?
An hourglass: a world of time entombed in yellow sand.

The Down There Narratives

Starring Veruca Salt, Pippi Longstocking, Cleopatra, Peppermint Patty,

Zuzu Bailey, Pocahontas, Scarlett O'Hara, Annie Chapman,

The Virgin Mary, Wonder Woman, Pebbles Flintstone,

Georgia O'Keefe, and Miss Piggy,

Queen Victoria, Foxy Brown

and Sappho

Following Years of Therapy, Cinderella Finally Let Go
of her Scullery Trauma and Remodels the Kitchen

Today the workmen come, demolish
and haul it all away—our showcase of macaroni
art, container of wiener and parsnip,

ossuary of roasted fowl, creamy chowder,
vessel of ice, sugar, mint. Our kitchen
ghosts dream of gingerbread petroglyphs,

specters of self-angled coho, pallet of candle,
resuscitator of olive, blackstrap and potion—
even the dough and scullery, the pudding,

force of crop, feast and pottage, breakers
of bread, coffee klatchers, even the collected
nest of wives. Where will they go after the fall?

Without the square meat hooks of your husband's
hands, without your godmother's blessings?
What past will they relinquish in this turbine

of familial territories, the circuitry in this holiest
of spaces? Our house's soul. Hearth of spirit.
This is the survivor of grease fire, expired milk,

pumpkin magic, mouse, lucky salt and candied beet.
Here, we sought reverie, fainted in pantries
and victory gardens. Here, we summoned

ancient Thanksgivings and pink frosted cakes.
We sacrificed spiders to the god of tea towels,
to the god of eggbeater and spoon, and re-anointed

in the name of granite countertops, and icebox idols
offered in colors of *ecru*, *pewter*, *bisque*.
Praise the mosaic backsplash, exalt and dance

to the disposal, speak to the alchemy of cupboard
space—Oh, happy Gladware, deliver us. Save the antique
toaster, multiple bottles of Ketchup, save the memories

and sweet tragedies, scent of fig and spoiled cheese—
home perms and boiled onion. Go gently
into that grand dumpster, refuse only the royal can know.

Interviews with the Carbon Gods

What of the pickle jar? Would it deserve
a fate more auspicious than a land-fill grave?
Would it welcome snakes, tadpoles or ants,
be happy with a bellyful of gold buttons
or as a vessel for marigolds?

> What of the egg carton? Does it not
> deserve an afterlife equal to its serviceable
> time above earth? Do I start my own flock
> to justify this elegantly crafted carton?
> Shall I save for a watchmaker's apprenticeship?

Alas, the paper-towel rod; peeled like an onion,
its lonely spine forlorn as a ham bone.
Weep for it. If an artist can create
an installation of fans, title it "Wind,"
then I name my eggshells, dryer lint,

> vacuum and teabag refuse
> "abandonment." My grandmother's ashes
> are sealed in a green vase on my aunt's mantel.
> Because my grandmother loved practical jokes
> I long to hijack them for folly and spite.

But unexpectedly, my uncle died and now his ashes
join my grandmother's. My plan lost
all allure as my aunt's house fills with the ashes
of dead people. If my grandmother's ashes
were mine, I'd plow them into the soil

of tomato plants, rows of blueberries
zucchinis, green beans, peas.
I'd anticipate the carbons of her ashes sprouting
dense, rich greens; the calcium of her bones
budding into flower, evolving into plump, amethyst-

bruised berries. I would freeze and can the surplus
so all winter she'd be called to memory
at every meal; her molecules transubstantiating
the labyrinths of my body, sustaining, nourishing,
renewing all the days of my life.

Is there practicality in the avocado pit?
Are the discarded clam shells currency or waste?
I am not an organ donor. I've made the tripe soup,
menudo. It is all honeycombed intestines
and the hooves of pigs. My grandmother saved

hair from her brushes and had them fashioned
into hair pieces. I keep a collection
of nail clippings from old lovers in case I ever indulge
in the black arts. Coiled inside a collectible
box, a legion of petrified spiders.

Rattlesnake rattles are very potent medicine.
Every day my grandfather burned our trash
in the rusty backyard barrel; I can still smell
the smoke, see the ash airborne against the sky.
My lover gifts me with beef hearts on Valentine's Day.

The day I was born, my father selected my name
from *Time* magazine. My namesake, a daredevil
woman who, outfitted in parachutes recycled
from old silks, flung herself from the wings
of airplanes into the vastness of rain forests.

II.

Winter

We assume Winter enters svelte and willow-limbed, a girl intimately acquainted with control, who cuts her chicken breast into quarter-inch segments, counts rice one grain at a time and pares down cauliflower to daisy-sized blooms.

But in fact, she reminds us of the pure cream and store-bought sugar the experts warn about: let's say the goat's cheese, the pillowy-soft flour rising with yeast. Let's say the white corn tortilla imprinted with the face of an angel. She believes in the curative properties of yogurt and the divinity of popped corn, just as she believes in the starch of clover honey and extracting the sore orange eye from the egg.

Her potato-thighs rub together when she walks, and her ass undulates like a surf of cottage cheese. And then there's the ice—not the striations of icicles appearing alongside rain-gutters like a row fangs, nor the wiry ribbons of frost sparked by glacial floats on the coldest day of the year, but snow globe and igloo facets cobbled in random disorder, sheets of crinoline and layers of taffeta, pale and downy, dimpled as sourdough at rest, fat as a prized luminary squash.

We would fail to pick her out from a line-up. We assume her thin as a paper cut, her spine the hook of a question mark, a heavily lined face. We might think she owns jack o'lantern's eyes or skin the pallor of chalk. But in fact, she defies these assumptions. She conserves heat like a jungle cat, flails her arms in the cloud-rink sky, rises to meet the sun in its golden-belly excess.

She has not been seduced for a decade: something about the matronly shape of her body, or maybe her laugh, which is raucous and high. When she glimpses her reflection in store-windows she sees herself as someone's maiden aunt stitched together with the last days of longing. But nothing about her reveals frigidity, even the smoke rings she presses out on idle, late afternoons, when she swings on the porch, bundled down in woolen throws, waiting for the burgeoning crocus, for the ice to break, waiting for the long-away arrival of spring.

Sex

Late March the stalking starts.
You say an ascension,
I say a salute.
You say dumb grab,
I second the sun. Mid-April
they reveal their one dark eye,
center-hot like a cinnamon bun.
The attractions begun,
the siren-calls, the color-lusting
whirs to scarlet
cleavage of petal,
amethyst-bruised mouths
sordid as chilies or patchouli,
poppy vivid. You say
never mind whose lips
are petticoat spread.
I say whose *what* is doing *that*
in particular *where.*
You say never mind the rain.
I say, oh yes, the rain.
The tulips make haste
in their gaudy sashes and slips,
pull their shutters closed,
abandon the doing *that*
in the certain *what* of it all.
A blue curtain falls
as the tulips droop.
You say a hothouse wilting,
lazily flapping.
I say winking idly in the drizzle,
pink heads bobbing,

flophouse, cathouse.
You say dipped and swirled,
a sputtering. I say a spilling,
a filling, in the rain,
in the rain. Not again.

The Girl with the Snake Tattoo

Evie snagged a rock star cruising Broadway—he was naked from the waist up except for the boa constrictor coiled around his neck like a reptile necklace. You can't get that at Tiffany's, except maybe in Vegas.

My best friend Evie, veritable street siren, mermaid without a tail, would flash her teeth, and men would suddenly appear, holding out red roses as if they'd just ripped them like freshly beating hearts from their chests. A shoulder shrug and the men would kneel and weep, sputtering out marriage proposals.

A few weeks earlier, Evie had snagged this dude—Phreddie Vomet, he called himself—claimed to be half Lakota, kept calling me Sis. He was in the middle of a hunger strike, all sharp angles, knife-y and frayed, the reason was unclear. He had an icicle-colored Mohawk and looked like a bedraggled rooster nobody wanted to fuck with; shaved off his eyebrows, his entire body from waist up covered in safety pins, pierced through his skin as if he was offering penance or fashioning a crude homage to a Plains Indian ceremony; as if the various parts of him were in danger of splitting apart, as if the seams and hems and darts of his body had begun to unravel and the safety pins were all that was holding him intact.

Evie got bored with him, quicker than usual. I felt badly for him when she set his car on fire—if he'd had a house, she would have set that on fire, so he actually got off easy. But Rex Temple, the snake guy, was different.

Evie was convinced they were forevermore, destined and star-crossed. I remember her saying they owed the universe to mix their helixes for the beautification of the world. I could see their spawn, each with identical copper hair and snakes coiled around their necks.

Evie wasn't used to falling, but she fell for this one. I'm certain it was the snake; I'm sure it put some kind of spell over her. Rex Temple seemed oblivious to the serpent's power. The snake would emanate testosterone and musky oils, its tongue issuing orange flickers of the divine, and I swear it talked; I swear it told Rex Temple everything to say like some kind of perverse ventriloquist.

Evie said that Rex Temple's brain was like a sieve, refusing to hold anything, and no matter how often you filled it, everything leaked out. But for some reason this never discouraged her from burning his name into her flesh with a hot needle. She preferred her lovers a little dumb. Once when he used the word "insinuate," she poked fun at him for days, "He's so cute, he actually used a multisyllabic word!" She thought it was riotous.

But, it was just the snake talking.

Rex Temple was a Grecian Lord in spandex and glam-rock hair.
The night it happened was during one of my parties: they'd spent hours in his car parked on the street in front of my house, right up until the sun rose, while I cleaned up beer cans and glasses, cigarette butts, retrieved snake shit from all over the carpet, under cushions. Evie's fish-netted legs were stuck out the passenger door, her hot pink stilettos dangling from her toes.

When she finally came inside, her face was amassed with amethyst-bruised kiss marks, her neck tracked with hickeys.

So, it didn't come as much of a surprise when one day she announced her pregnancy test strip had turned blue. And she was thrilled. She danced around the apartment singing "It's blue, it's blue, it's blue!" I was worried. Turns out, with reason.

Rex Temple disappeared, poof, vanished into the air like a fart, and nine months later, Evie bore a litter of perfectly formed serpents, five of them, each a finger on the long hand of fate. Five snakes, their pink tongues orbiting the moon of Evie's nipple in search of nectar and dreams.

Evening Meal

Mushrooms are seekers.
They sweat in a pan of garlic and butter,
fuss, bicker and toss—
toughing it out like the rest of us.
They furl, tucking into themselves
along an arm of steam.
They eye a slant of vinegar, the crush
of lemon rising like a halved sun
along horizon of skillet.
And all because they want
what we want:
the dose of salt, the kiss, to be poured
onto a plate. They want praise,
perhaps even dare, ask for love.

Voracious Insatia

Ravenous for the printed word, she consumes books.

In the beginning it was benign: brochures, IKEA catalogues, ticker-tape—kid stuff—and within a short time she developed a taste for phonebooks, the yellow pages or restaurant listings were her favorite.

Soon she graduated to the public library, and after they revoked her card, she still crept past the page and ensconced herself in the remotest niche—the sections no one ever visited, like the foreign translations and mechanical engineering. She ingested pages of Mishima in Japanese and obscure physics' equations till she was so stuffed she thought she might die.

Did they quell? Did they satisfy?

Sometimes she craves Latin literature: *One Hundred Years of Solitude* or something by Borges. Their stories slide so gracefully down her throat, hot and salty like the humidity that had made her faint while kneeling at the Mexico City Cathedral. Their stories remind her of the shop girl singing *Paper Roses* along to the radio—sometimes spicy, sometimes just a lick of cinnamon.

Or sometimes she craves the Beats. It is always the music that takes her first, a transport to a dark address. She leans back into it, flings her body to its Buddhist heart, takes Charlie Parker, the rambling incoherencies of Kerouac and Cassady, the lusty howls of Ginsberg on a rooftop, Burroughs sleeping it off in Tangiers and it is all about that syncopation, that percussion, that... sex.

She dips those pages in brine, in sweet-and-sour sauce, Tabasco and molasses. It is more than desire, more than hunger. She wants transcendence, she wants enlightenment. When Dylan Thomas raged against the dying of the light she raged too. When Sethe smashed her baby's skull, she tasted both the sweet freedom of release and the shackling of a woman's spirit. When Scout discovered the true meaning behind the mockingbird's plight and Atticus righted a society's injustice, she sandwiched the righteousness like bread and butter, ate it whole, crusts and all.

She wants those words. She wants those liturgies, those witnesses, those gospels. She combs those truths through her hair like honey rinse—sweet and brittle on her tongue and warm in her stomach like baked apples, like knowledge.

Letter from Your Child's School Regarding the Fall
Production of *Pumpkin Splice Girls the Musical*

Dearest Parent,

On behalf of Dahlhause School for Young Ladies, I am very pleased to announce this year's fall production will be *Pumpkin Splice Girls, the Musical* produced by our very own Savage Lord of Autumnus, with music by Redrum Redrum. We've got some extra special surprises this year, what with equinox just around the corner, and we are writing today to let you know that the production crew is looking for a few good acolytes, so reply at your earliest convenience, ~~pyres~~ positions are going fast! We would also appreciate any financial contributions you might be able to manage, as we are needing to rebuild part of the stage due to last year's snafu with the production of *Little Wicker Women*. Who knew that bubble wrap was so flammable!

You may be familiar with Savage Lord of Autumnus from previous school events; we submitted to his dark arts the year the crops were failing and it behooved us to repay him with the blood of a virgin, so we're pretty much locked in now. But don't get me wrong, the students and faculty just love having him slithering around, and he was a big hit at our last carwash fundraiser, boy howdy! The things a pumpkin headed daemon can do with invoking the Winds of Temptation to insta-quick-dry a Range Rover is really a sight to behold.

We're quite proud of *Pumpkin Splice Girls the Musical* and consider ourselves lucky to be presenting it. Of course, Savage Lord of Autumnus pulled some strings for the production rights, but what good is being a supernatural entity if you can't reap a few benefits. Speaking of reaping, we hope that you will take time out this year to buy tickets for our special raffle, where we have big plans for Mrs. Rena, our resident lunch lady, involving some WD40 and a spool of mortal coil.

Please sign the attached permission slip and return it as soon as possible. We take pride in our theater program here at Dahlquist's School for Young Ladies, and hope that your daughter will be considered ebullient and luminous enough to participate in our latest production. We always emphasize that there are no small roles, only small actors, and sometimes when you're lucky, there's small animals, such as goats, involved as well. Savage Lord of Autumnus has terrific instincts about such things. We understand he performed in *Terminator vs Predator, the Opera*.

Just one last thing: Savage Lord of Autumnus wishes to extend his reckoning glee with the following message, which we're passing along to you: "We are preparing the cornfield, constructing the pyre, bring me your daughters, we sacrifice virgins at dawn." Isn't he a hoot!

Yours Sincerely,

Principal Anita Minon

Erotica Writing Workshop Imagined

1. "I thought it was overly cliché, especially the heteronormative aspects."

2. "A pizza delivery girl? Why can't she be a cable technician or a plumber?"

3. "But logistically, her feet can't literally be wrapped around her ears, unless she's Gumby."

4. "That's inherently sexist."

5. "Sex IS sexist."

6. "There's too much 'gasping' and 'sighing'; how about a nice 'sputter' on occasion."

7. "So, you're saying the tribbles were actually little vaginas multiplying exponentially? That's messed up."

8. "Stilettos on or stilettos off? I don't want to say I'm speaking from experience, but they aren't good dildos, just saying."

9. "I can't keep track of who's doing what to whom—can you cut some pronouns?"

10. "Is the lubricant biodegradable?"

11. "Is the condom dolphin safe?"

12. "Are the edible panties gluten-free?"

13. "Wait, who's the speaker? I assumed it was a personal memoir, baby."

14. "I don't get why he'd spit on it first considering she's described as 'a ready-ripe plum.'"

15. "This seems to be stealing from Anais Nin."

16. "Were 19th Century Native Americans cut or uncut, because Red Wolf sounds circumcised."

17. "I know it's a circus, but it's really offensive to little people."

18. "I doubt a Tyrannosaurus Rex could even reach that far while boinking at the same time."

19. "You know in some cultures mustaches on women are attractive."

20. "Men shouldn't throw women to the ground and rip their clothes off, even if her eyes are 'alighted with fury and lust.'"

21. "Why can't the babysitter be male?"

22. "Technically that's impossible unless he used Viagra."

23. "You're mixing your metaphors too generously—speeding trains AND champagne corks popping is a bit heavy-handed."

24. "Did Trilliem Delight see stars or fireworks? Also, can sex robots orgasm?"

25. "The ending wasn't very surprising."

Lipstick For Jesus

Yesterday, it was some random
book title, HONOR,
eyes going, I misread HORNY.
Today, driving through
traffic, scores of picketers
brandishing signs, I muse
out loud as we wait for the light
to change—ADOPTION STOPS
A BEATING HEART. That's weird,
I say. And you say, Need new glasses, much?
It's A B O R T I O N.
Oh. I say, that makes better sense.
And again at the drugstore,
you find me stock still
puzzling out a makeup display
that reads JESUS' GIRL.
I like that, I say, lipstick for
Jesus, mascara for Christ.
You say, Um, no it's J E S S E 'S GIRL.
Who is Jesse? I say,
I dunno, you say, maybe that song?
Weird, I say. Another display:
SCOPE OUTLAW.
You correct me, SCOPE O U T L A S T S.
And so, that's how life's been
going lately. I'm Ms. Magoo,
misprints far and wide, Mercury
in perpetual retrograde, the world
all at once pious and fugitive—
just a little bit of danger
lying in wait, everywhere.

My Father's Mistress

The fashionable ones he placed
on exhibit in the living room
next to his Atlas and Collier's
Encyclopedias, like a courtesan
placed in the chambers of lords.
The virgins got stacked in the top drawer
above Mother's hankies and pinafores,
for easy access. While the used were discarded,
passed around to the boys, or else languished
on the shelf having lost their luster,
their pluck, their strut, shit out of luck.
Every free moment of his life
my father made love to books.
In the bathroom, in the lounge, at the table,
in the bed, in the bed, in the bed,
he'd lose his head, his youth, his wife,
his life, all for a good play, a murder mystery,
a history of Greece, a Mark Twain chuckle,
he'd suckle any strumpet as long as she had ink,
a spine and made you think,
or not. She got every inch of his attention,
be it potboiler, tome, digest or novel,
oh, she was a marvel, he succumbed to her spell
regardless the lessons she taught,
high-brow or low, he'd take her fast
or take her slow, make her last,
all night through. The mornings after
we'd find him sprawled out, spent,
with his mistress consumed,
her pages all bent.

Sixth Street House Sonnet #1

Jenny is toothless, eyeless, and hairless.
She spits puh-puh-puh-puh-puh-puh-puh-puh,
like a snare drum, a cough, choke fit, a mess.
She's small, barely four feet tall and she loves
us all except when she doesn't. At meals,
applesauce orbits her mouth, Jenny's hands
astound, she sculpts food into mushy balls,
then climbs and spiders the halls, rubberbands
from one lap to next, extorts wet kisses
from staff. Jenny's a woman with the mind
of a babe, she seizes, she smacks, misses
nothing, lives in a shroud among her kind:
Cindy's radio and Jane's dementia,
all surrounded by vivid absentia.

Sixth Street House Sonnet #2

Jenny's blind, Lara's deaf, perfect roomies, one
burns the lights all night and the other sings
along to her radio, claps her hands
to *Thriller* and sometimes Celine Dion.

Their room looks like what I would imagine
they might imagine their insides to be,
like the cavities of Teddy bears, see
pink, see plush, see clowns waiting to happen—

whirling and wild carnivals with rainbow
unicorns and cupcakes to eat all day
long! Lara dips her hands into tableau
glass beads, colors dart every which way

throughout the room which Jenny cannot see
except for their assault striking her cheek.

Sixth Street House Sonnet #3

The women are mostly tiny, like dolls,
a blessing for their caretakers who rack
them into their wheelchairs to cruise the mall's
artificial light and droning muzak

which I'd name Hymns for the Inheritors
of the Earth and for every milestone gained—
less tantrums, less seizures, improved motor
skills, spoon holding, self fed, self toilet trained—

put a gold star on the chart and give praise,
praise, praise! Jenny's nixed her Depends, Cindy
quit stripping down at Winco's Grocery,
Anne swapped helmet for a gait harness. Pray

for the meek, for each small triumph they reap.
Modest earthlings, little birds beyond sweet.

Distracted from COVID-19, Attention Shifts
to MIA Maiden from Land O'Lakes Butter Box

America mourns for the Indian
figure who knelt like a supplicant before dairy,
fatly blessed our milks, our cheeses,

anointed our lands & shores.
The Google tutorials surface—
the "boob trick": score the box & fold to make

a window for her knees to jut through.
O our butter maiden
brought all the boys to the yard.

Twittersphere so prostrate with grief
petitions are launched for the Dairy Princess:
O our pat O Americana,

O our dab O Disneyesque,
O our dollop O Heritage.
The mourning procession bears witness:

Jolly Green Giant & Chicken of the Sea Mermaid,
Uncle Ben & Aunt Jemimah,
magically delicious leprechaun & Peter Pan—

even the Argo Cornstarch Maiden & Mazola
Margarine "you call it corn, we call it maize"
spokesIndian raise stalks in solidarity.

Mia, aptly named, our butter girl mascot,
the only Indian woman gone missing
that anyone notices, anyone cares about.

Indigenous Census Statistics

Approximately 70 percent of American Indians and Alaska Natives live in urban areas. –Department of Health and Human Services Office of Minority Health (2017)

1:: seventy percent of native americans live in cities

2:: sixty-two percent live in converted lofts with floors refurbished from mid-western church doors

3:: nineteen percent reside in re-purposed urns crafted by trappist monks

4:: forty-seven percent live in tri-level modern industrial condos

5:: eleven percent live in lighthouses along the eastern seaboard

6:: thirty-five and a half percent live in narwhal caves

7:: two percent live in hemlock and pine high-rises of northern idaho

8:: thirteen percent live in subterranean dugouts in siberia

9:: five percent live in reimagined beehive colonies

10:: fifty-seven percent live in abstract liminal spaces conjured by soothsayers and druids

:Sheltering:

a: You are chopping onions for yet another pot of lentils, hips pressed
up against the kitchen counter, when first you hear
it. The sound of mewling. Barely audible. You put down your
knife.

b: One year earlier, on fellowship in Kansas, you are returning to your
Airbnb from your walk. You see your house and yard down
the street within view, but something looks peculiar. As you come
closer you can make it out: a vulture feeding on a possum's corpse.

c: Plague doctors of 17th century Europe wore black masks that
resembled the beaks of birds.

a: It sounds like a kitten in distress. So, you turn to open the front door,
to step barefoot up a slab of concrete stairs and scan the yard, the
street, the park across the way. The mewling again, you tip your
head back and see it.

d: Researchers proposed bats as the most likely reservoir for
SARS-CoV-2. However, there are no documented cases of direct bat-
human transmission.

e: In the months before your mother's death, an owl visited her back
patio for several days in a row. There are many ways to interpret this.

b: The dead possum is in your yard, just steps away from your bedroom
window. How long has the possum been there? As you move closer the
vulture is spooked and flies away.

c: The half-foot long "beaks" of these sinister looking masks were filled
with perfumes and herbs. It was commonly thought that perfumes
and fragrant herbs protected the wearer from diseases. The medicine
of the time believed that the black plague was contracted through
poisoned air. The perfumes were thought to fumigate the air.

d: This suggests that an intermediate host between bats and humans
was involved. The research also suggests that SARS-CoV-2 is
similar to strains of bird flu.

a: A black bird. In the top branches of the tree in your yard. It is making
a fuss, about what you can't begin to know. Except that the similarity
between "Corvid" — a class of birds, among them crows and ravens —
and "Covid" isn't lost on you.

e: Today, Waubgeshig Rice, the author, posted that "the crow is black
and can only say "kaa." Which is the Ojibwe word for 'no.'"

b: The day before the dead possum and vulture, you visited KU's
butterfly sanctuary. Monarchs migrate to warmer climes just like
birds. They can travel from fifty to a hundred miles a day. You observed
newly born butterflies in a wall-to-wall cage. Their collective sound —
wings *flupping*; a rushing pulse of air.

Re-Writing the Great American (Indian) Novel:
   Classics Edition

On the (Good Red) Road

The grandfather of *Powwow Highway* and *Smoke Signals*, this classic post-war, road novel is an Indian tour de force that features the modern lives of the (Drum)Beat Generation as they drive into the heart of "America."

The Bilagáana Jar

Meet Esther Yazzie; she won a scholarship to intern at *Seventeen Magazine* in big city Manhattan. Her sanity is tested to the brink, however, as she soon realizes she is the only Navajo in New York. Will she stay and bear it out? Or will she ride the bus back home to the rez?

Valley of the (Kachina) Dolls

Welcome to Santa Fe, the hot zone for the widespread epidemic of New Age tourists, culture vultures and plastic medicine men, and their addiction to Southwestern Indian culture.

The Dreamcatcher in the Rye

Alienation from mainstream society is a prevalent theme in Native American fiction, and *The Dreamcatcher in the Rye* highlights that sense of discomfort and distance while also depicting the tortured angst of adolescence.

True Facts!

True Fact: Did you know that *The Deer Hunter, Apocalypse Now* and *Full Metal Jacket* were originally screenplays about Native American men going into military service? But the producers insisted on whitewashing the characters to appear more universally acceptable for large audiences? The role played by Meryl Streep was originally written as a Lenape woman, but it was decided to make her and the rest of the community Russian Orthodox.

True Fact: While the old school classics (whoopie cushion, huckleberry cream pie in the face) are pretty cheesy by today's standards, back in the day they were comedy gold! It was Sitting Bull who originated the Takes My Wife please schtick and in a 1967 *Newsweek* interview, the famous King-Of-The-One-Liners comic Henny Youngman credits Sitting Bull as being his inspiration for comedy. "Sitting Bull was my comedy spirit patronus," Youngman said.

True Fact: It is not widely known that the legendary Hunkpapa leader Sitting Bull, Tȟatȟáŋka Íyotake, was a notorious practical joker. He often pranked Red Cloud during tribal council by placing a whoopie cushion beneath Red Cloud's buffalo robe with hilarious results! But he stole all of his best material from the band's heyoka, Pretty Wallowing Woman, and passed it off as his own.

Indigenous Erasure Poem

Savage Ghazal

Wigwam-rhetoric, Hiawatha-speak, Gitchigoomie *Savage*
this, savage that. Gag me with a coup stick. Savage

literature for masses. Unbelievable—Barbie doll
in buckskin, a scarlet-haired, green-eyed Poca-ho savage

straight from a Land O'Lakes butter box, call
her fake like Tomahawk Tassels' savage

burlesque show in Minneapolis, that girl who fell
from grace, fell in love with kitsch, like the *Savage*

Series romances sold world-wide, *Dances with Schmiel,*
Dances with Schmazel. Synopses are neat! Start with *Savage*

Spirit : Kickapoo Chief Fire Thunder (for real)
rescues his kidnapped sister from the circus side-show! *Savage*

Heat : Zoe Hawkins lusts after Kiowa brave White Shadow, all
taboo, of course, what's passion if not forbidden, if not savage?

Another : Morning Hawk, crazy in love for a Mohawk she'd kill
for—naturally, an Indian maiden will cut a bitch, savage-

hearted they are, especially Apaches, they trill
at the sight of blood. Take the southwestern saga, *Savage*

Arrow : High Hawk and Rising Moon both love a white girl
with flame-red hair. Always with the gingers! Savage-

hearted as Indians on the prairie and almost as criminal!
Take Yvonne, whose lust's ignited by Silver Arrow in *Savage*

Passion : dark storms and treachery, a virile (viral)
stranger sets blood afire, trembling like a fawn. In *Savage*

Torment : our heroine-in-heat sets out to steal
the heart of fierce Strong Hawk, a forest savage

of the Michigan woodlands, her daddy owns the mill—
they're star-crossed but doomed. Rinse and repeat. *Savage*

rhymes with *new age* and that's another kind of swill—
another bitter pill to swallow, savage

stomach indigestion. Guilty pleasures' appeal,
sure, but in the final analysis, its lure's all atrocity, all savage.

III.

Horns

1. Our Father Who Art in Heaven

I do not believe in god.
      Belief is a word stricken from the family tongue.
            We do not believe in anything,

Father commandeers from the head
      of the table, his snout pressing out odious,
            black vapor. I want more than anything

to challenge him; I want to shout
      to believe in disbelief IS believing!
            But voicing the obvious is useless.

I know what kind of belief he's referring to,
      and I could froth and spit,
            convulse or spin my head around like a top

all for naught. For my father, god doesn't exist,
      "belief" is a perverse word,
            and any mention of either results in typhoons,

earthquakes or chronic stomach indigestion.
      He is an intellectual virtuoso, but a sore loser.
            He is selective about his truths, and he is recklessly proud—

he is the devil after all.

2. Safari

"Even the devil gets lonely." This has become my father's credo, his mantra. Before he plotted to impregnate and marry my mother, he toured the earth over, entertained himself as a Hemingway incarnate, mated with elephants, giraffes, zebras and lions. Animals of the African savannah gave him a thrill, appealed to his grandiosity, his penchant for the exotic. "The larger the better," he'd say, sucking on his cigar. "But a woman will do in a pinch." I noticed Mother knitting her brows together, a familiar shadow passing over her face. Her chagrin amused Father as he snorted blue smoke throughout the room.

3. Ox-blood Martinis

I was a divine accident,
product of a few-too-many ox-blood martinis.
Father sabotaged his plans for a boy

by getting dreadfully ripped.
Only male spawn makes a proper demon, he spit.
His litany of excuses:

an exhausting day appointing tyrannical
world leaders; evangelist
ministers to lead astray; bad monkey brains

for dinner, and yes, he was drunk.
So, they got me, a girl. Mother was over the moon
of course, but Father took months, *years*

overcoming his regret. Being Satan naturally
makes him the worst of misogynists.
To his mind, a girl-child is tantamount to impotence.

He wanted to name me Bathsheba.
But Mother insisted no one could spell it,
that such a name would only stigmatize

me. I was nearly branded Marquis
after *the* Marquis, you know de Sade? Who's
been Father's bowling partner for years,

my godfather to boot. But Mother put her foot down,
a French name's too pretentious. Why Ruth then?
I can't imagine. But Ruth it became. Perhaps

because there was no looking back. Not ever.

4. Hollywood Exploitation

The year Hollywood made a movie
based on our lives was the year my mother
started seeing her analyst five times a week.

She carried her outrage around
like a travel pack of Kleenex in her purse—
conveniently located and oft retrieved.

Mia Farrow looks nothing like me. Mother liked
to believe she resembled a better-looking Jacqueline Kennedy,
in fact, in her more despairing moments

she lamented her misfortune in not being *the* First Lady herself:
I could have had him. My cotillion was just as lavish.
And she can't decorate worth shit,

she wouldn't know a damask from a toile if they bit her on her bony ass.
Mother also ranted about Hollywood being corrupted
by crews of male, chauvinistic, capitalistic pigs.

Can you believe the temerity of them
to reinvent you as a boy? A boy? Is it so unimaginable Satan's
spawn is a girl? They're all swine I tell you, legions

of demon swine looking for warm bodies to occupy.
Neither of us dared to speak the truth:
Father was Hollywood's mogul.

5. Broken Homes

Mother's been seeing a Jungian analyst on Park Avenue.
Last week, breading bat wings for dinner,
she announced to Father that Dr. Beetle suggested they divorce.
She said she couldn't take it anymore, that he was never home,
and when he was, all he did was watch television.
She complained she was sick of his tantrums,
she thought he was more interested in corrupting
the universe than spending quality time with his family.
And the last thing—he was a lousy lay. That did it.
Father stormed from the apartment vowing
never to return, while Mother took a bottle
of Vodka to bed and stayed up all night weeping
and phoning her old Vassar dorm sisters.

> *Oh Buffy, whoever would want me now?*
> *If I left him what suitor in his right mind*
> *would ever come near me? I'm not exactly*
> *a debutante anymore.*

She persisted through the night,
calling everyone in her alumni book, cataloguing
every argument, every betrayal.

> *That's what I said, Binky. An orangutan.*
> *How could I invent something that profane,*
> *that lascivious? That bitch shed orange hair*
> *all over my duvet, I wasn't imagining it.*

> *I'll tell you Kitty, if I had to do it over again*
> *I would have married Skip Westhoff. I don't imagine*
> *it would have occurred to him to barbecue poor uncle Tank.*

I mean what kind of barbarian assumes a family picnic
means to eat actual members of the family?

"When he's excited it points due north,
when he's not excited it points due north—the son-of-a-bitch
is a living compass, twenty-four hours a day.
And it's so huge, where am I living, the Redwood National
    Forest?
I may as well have married a Clydesdale.

His saying that I am as sexy as the Goddess
of Fertility is NOT a compliment,
and I don't care how many times he fucked her!

I don't care if leather is the appropriate token
for a three-year anniversary, and NO it wasn't
a romantic gesture. The bastard exhumed
my grandmother and made her into a riding crop.

That's what I said, Bunny, his death is an absolute
impossibility, so forget your gardener's cousin Vito,
no hit man in the world could take him out. What
part of immortal don't you understand?

Hello . . . may I speak to Senator Westhoff?

6. Sugar and Spice

In the beginning, Father anticipated
his offspring to live
up to his own rotten image of himself.
Mother scolded him
for this idea—called him a narcissist,
and reminded him
of a certain someone whom he despised.
This reference shut him up—
the most subtle allusion to the big-G
usually did. I had
to hand it to her, Mother had a knack
for calming the beasts
within. But when credit was due
she was obstinately humble.

"It was the horns that did it." She said, as if her strategies carried no
    weight.
"The day you began sprouting horns was the day your father finally
    accepted you."

It might have been true, horns
making a difference.
But her references to evil women
throughout history
and legend might have influenced
my father as well.
"Aren't females trickier? Inherently
more conniving
than males?" She asked Father
who'd been sulking
the last three days (an incorrigible

mood triggered
by his crony Sleestak, whose wife
had just given birth
to a litter of crocodilian serpents—
male crocodilian serpents).

Father fixed his yellow slits into the garden of my mother's face, put down
his newspaper and pondered her question. He didn't answer her,
but it shifted the brain stem nonetheless.

Another time Mother said, "Don't you admire the black widow?
Isn't it lovely how she devours
her mate after union? Wasn't she your invention, Dear?"
To this, Father grinned,
acutely proud at himself. Father's resistance wasn't a reflection
of whether I was worthy of love.
His initial resistance had more to do with his own flawed values
(an understatement if there ever was one),
coupled with his overwhelming sense of failure—a failure
that cut him so deep
he hasn't attempted to procreate again.

The laws of the universe are not absolute, nor are they limitless; if Father
ever gains the courage to *try- try again*, the universe will surely be in his
corner. But should he fail—that is, within his own misogynistic "logic"—
and sire another female, that would be an event in which he'd surely
perish.

He is corrupt, but also pure. He is *nearly* omnipotent,
but his ego is weak.

And should he cease, the world as we know it would disappear
along with him,
for without evil, there is no balance. If I had been male,
I'd have been a protégé,
and expected to make my own black stain on this world—
as well as the one of darkness
and shadows. And despite my being half human, the half
mother says is my best half,
I would have been an exemplary pupil of evildoing, excelling
in all enclaves of anarchy and wickedness.

The nature of humans has always been a bone of contention between my
mother and father. Mother is firm in her belief that humans are kind, polite
and good natured, but she grew up in Connecticut; she had pony parties
and engraved invites to supper clubs. Father, of course, thinks humans are
treacherous, selfish, and immoral—which is why he spends so much time
on earth, he feels right at home.

My babyish charms won him over in time,
for those were some of the better days, the salad days,

and our family album is overflowing
with photos presenting a buoyant

and contented portrait of family life—
albeit one mired in peculiarity,

but Mother often compared us
with the growing number of mixed-race families

cropping up like microwave ovens across the country.
She comforted herself with that similarity,

often stating how progressive and worldly a woman
she'd turned out to be; how sophisticated and broad minded she was—

and then she'd pour herself another cocktail, or hop a train
down to the Village for her mixed-race marriage support group.

She told herself what she needed to believe,
in order to draw the curtains and face the world every afternoon.

> *Their family snapshots are an endearing testimony*
> *to the poignancy within the bonds of family,*
> *the impressions of which, left an indelible mark*
> *upon me. I am most grateful to the DeMones*
> *for sharing their compelling family archive.*

A quote from none other than Norman Rockwell himself,
after he was commissioned to paint our portraits

for the anniversary edition of *Life* magazine.
There's an odd mix to our snapshots:

Father reading me Edgar Allan Poe tales at bedtime;
clamming on Cape Cod; Mother spoon-feeding me goat's blood formula;

excursions into the garden to bait slugs;
my first fang; sand castles at Fire Island;

hunting Trumpeter swans upstate;
picking crab apples in Vermont;

the underworld's annual carnival;
sword fishing with Papa Hemingway;

me, in the North Pole, sitting on Santa's knee;
Mother and Father getting blotto at a New Year's Eve party;

barrel-riding at Niagara Falls;
my controversial first day in public school;

carving Halloween jack o'lanterns;
our family vacation to Auschwitz.

Mr. Rockwell insisted we were a delight to capture on canvas! That I was
the prettiest gargoyle he'd ever seen! His work of art has a place of honor
above our fireplace: Mother's soft, glowing features, and lovely form are a
stark contrast to Father's fiendish demeanor and my decidedly impish
countenance. The painting doesn't stray far from the reality of our daily
lives:

The Dark Father Knows Best

Father is sucking on a pipe in front of the fire
browsing the daily news;
Mother is bent over the coffee table, serving a tray
of bloody Marys and canapés;
I am perched at Father's feet, absorbed in combing
a Barbie doll's hair.
The only inconsistencies? Father prefers cigars and none
of my dolls have hair.

7. Girl Scouts of America

Grasped in my slick claws,
two cases of Girl Scout cookies.
Mother is trying to attach the beret to my head—
she swears under her breath because last night
she attended one of her consciousness-raising
meetings and from her attitude today
she appears to have raised her consciousness—
about three gin and tonics worth before noon.

"Oh, let's just take this thing off, it's not going to stay put." She says, exasperated. "No, Mother," I say, "here, look." I take scissors and cut two equally-sized holes through the top of the beret, then fitting my horns through the holes, place the beret atop my head. "Does it look alright?" She replies in a weary tone, "I don't know why I didn't think of that."

Father has been gone since last week.
Mother says that even though he's burdensome
to have slithering around the apartment,
stubbing out cigars on the credenza
and breaking dishes under his hooves
she can't get along without him.
It has something to do with his being her master
even though part of her recoils at the very idea.
Last week she said, "I'm no different than other women.
Gloria Steinem thinks all men are devils."

The reason Father isn't here is because he and Mother had a terrible fight. "What's gotten into you, woman!" Father raged, knocking over the Tiffany lamp with his tail. "No spawn of mine is going to be a do-gooder Girl Scout!"

Mother having fortified herself with a pitcher
of margaritas stood her ground.
"It's about time Ruth made some normal friends—
not those winged monkeys
and condemned souls you bring around!
She needs to be with real girls!"
Real girls. Like Pinocchio.
Father reared up on his hooves,
as if he were going to crush her,
but instead scorched the davenport tassels—
hot kernels of flame sputtering from his throat.
"A Girl Scout, Rosemary?
What sort of values will that instill?"

Mother crossed her arms over her chest, not backing down, while Father
hovered over her, his eyes shining like flashlight beams. He knew he was
beat. In a final act of defiance, he snorted, "Is there no evil left in the world!
Next, she'll be volunteering for the Red Cross!"

Then he transformed
into a hundred-and-one small black birds,
the raucous applause of their collective wings
like an exhaust of wild and terrible smoke
escaped through the windows.
We haven't seen him since.
Mother said not to worry—
that he'd return. He always did.

8. Demonica and Chaotica

Chaotica runs her blood red nails down
the length of my Partridge Family poster
while her wretched sister, Demonica, pilfers
through my ballerina jewelry box.

Chaotica picks up my slinky from the bureau,
stretches the wires effortlessly,
they break apart cleanly in one place.
She molds the slinky around her neck,
resembling one of those ostrich deities
from the Necropolis Abyss. Father brought
them home as pets. Before it was Oompa Loompas,
then mermaids. It was always something.

"Yeah, well… my mother pinned it up,"
I say, my voice tremulous and thin sounding.
"You know how humans are… heh heh."
The sisters both gawk at me

with identically snide and dubious expressions.
"Oh, yes, *humans*," Demonica sneers.
"Such pathetic creatures. I don't know
how you stand to have one for a mother but then… oops!"

She feigns dismay. "Gee, I beg your pardon, Ruthie,
I forget… you're *half*," Chaotica snorts.
I could easily serve up these two bitches
into lunchmeat sandwiches and use their tongues

for toothpick garnishes but their father
is a valuable minion in my father's army.
His name is Decarabia, the sixty-ninth spirit

87

who governs the 66 Legions.

He is the invoker of winds and his daughters'
mothers are the Winds of Peril and Temptation.
Besides being invaluable to my father
in a professional capacity, Decarabia is also a dear friend,

so, when it comes to Chaotica and Demonica,
I have to eat shit and practice the self-control
of a Sabnock Master. Ordinarily I would have total dominion
over them and ordinarily they would yield to my position,

being who my father is, of course,
except it's true, my mother's blood diminishes my position.
And at least, for the time being, I am impotent
and have been sternly warned by Father

not to so much as lift a finger of harm towards them.
But my thoughts are wicked. And I vow one day
they will know the taste of their own intestines.
"Milk and cookies, anyone?"

Mother pops her head into the doorway.
She is carrying a tray and sets it on my school desk.
"How are you girls doing? How are your mothers?
I should phone them. Will you send them my regards?"

Mother is such a phony.
She can't stand Peril and Temptation,
but they always volunteer for the school fundraiser
every year so she works to keep up appearances.

"Yes, Mrs. DeMone, we'd be glad to pass that on."
The girls cheerfully proclaim in stereo.

9. Late Night Television

Tonight, is a very special evening,
Father is the distinguished guest on Johnny Carson.

When he trotted out to greet Johnny
the whole audience booed —

but you could tell
Father was really appreciative of the reception.

Mother sat with her needlepoint,
"isn't your father handsome tonight?"

I nodded my head in agreement,
but in truth I thought not —

actually, Father is quite hideous.
There must be more than a little truth

to the expression, *love is blind,*
although some days he's better than others.

He can shapeshift on command,
but he also has a salamander-like response to stimuli.

I haven't inherited the former
although I do possess a kind of involuntary twitch

that unnerves my mother who reacts
as if I just farted on a crowded elevator.

The majority of the time,
my father's looks are just what you'd expect

a demonic prince to look like:
a ruddy complexion, horny and slope-headed,

a severe and elongated chin
so sharply pointed he looks like an ice pick,

an interstate of ridges and scars wandering
in erratic patterns across his head and face,

disquieting eyes that change colors
according to the weather of his moods,

epidermis the texture of a diamondback,
and musculature that resembles a nylon stuffed with grapefruits.

And then there's the wings—
those godforsaken wings:

scabby and moth-eaten draperies
hooked lopsided to his backside like a third-world circus tent.

Johnny Carson addresses Father,
"You've been known to move things with your mind,

spew fire, smoke and vapor,
heck, you can fly faster than a Pan Am Express to Acapulco!"

This comment garners some hearty laughs
from the audience. "You're what they call a renaissance man,

because really, is there anything you can't do?"
In addition to the shapeshifting,

I have inherited many of Father's
other attributes as well—although to a lesser degree.

My wings for instance, by comparison,
are mere nubs and very tidy.

And my horns, smaller than a musk ox's
but bigger than a Luciferian cherub's,

are likely to catch up to Father's with each passing year.
My father's heinous appearance

troubled him a great deal, in the beginning.
He was once *the* perfect model of beauty,

but his beauty wasn't what you'd say
about a merely handsome figure,

as in, *there goes a tall drink of water,* or,
that guy is sure easy on the eyes.

No, my father was beautiful as in a shining
beam of light so dazzling you had to shield your eyes.

He was resplendent, shimmering;
they called him Morning Star and Shining One.

His being reduced from such exalted proportions
to so grotesque a beast that babies cried, and people recoiled

in horror at the sight of him, was a tremendous blow
to his ego, to say the least.

However, he's had thousands of years to get over it,
and now merrily revels in it.

In fact, he's disappointed if an old lady
doesn't keel over from heart arrest,

or his shadow doesn't peel the paint off the walls.
We used to play an amusing game when I was little,

where Father would sneak up and "surprise"
the new maids (we go through housekeepers

quicker than you can say, Mr. Clean),
and they'd shriek and hit the tile,

and I'd go running down the hall
after the smelling salts howling like a banshee.

It was really fun. Mother would come
positively unglued by our antics,

admonishing us for losing
so many housekeepers time and time again.

I was blissfully unaware of my own wretched
appearance up until the time I started public school.

Sure, I had noticed a time or two when pedestrians
squealed and bolted like frightened deer

on a country road, but my appearance
was more endearing than horrific.

For one thing, my mother is a stunning woman,
so, I had that in my favor.

And secondly, my looks—though appreciably rough
around the edges—have a particularly rugged chic,

an enigmatic quality often akin to mythical deities,
and high school gym teachers.

And then there's the hybridity,
my inter-species-ness—if you will.

There is something strangely compelling
about a cross breeding of species;

you see it in flower gardens,
and it's visible in dog shows.

What was once two ordinary parts, come together,
fusing the most formidable essences of each,

and yielding results that are unquestionably unique,
and perhaps even superior.

Hybrid vigor. I should clarify, however,
that not all interbreeding is auspicious:

Dr. Moreau's little science experiments, for instance.
Not a pretty outcome

and one doomed to failure and carnage from the get-go.
Although, the downfall of the island

probably had less to do with his precious vivisections
and more to do with the reckless folly of his god-like ambitions.

God is great but don't fuck with him.
I'm destined to co-exist with such legacies

for the rest of my immortal days.
Aberrant combinations can and do occur

within natural conditions;
it's the righteous order of things.

But for mortals like Dr. Moreau
and certain Frankensteins and Jekylles

working in armored laboratories in the Netherlands,
such experiments are perilous.

Mother leaned forward from her chair
and adjusted the television.

"Do you think Father looks ten pounds heavier?
I don't believe what they say about that."

I was feeling sleepy from my cocoa,
"Father looks fine," I told her.

I would have liked to have stayed awake
for the whole program but I fell asleep

right about the time Johnny was cracking jokes
about offering himself as a human sacrifice.

Tiffany Midge is a citizen of the Standing Rock Sioux Nation and was raised by wolves in the Pacific Northwest. Her work has appeared in *The New Yorker*, *The Brooklyn Rail*, *First American Art Magazine*, *World Literature Today*, *McSweeney's*, and more. Midge's previous poetry collection *The Woman Who Married a Bear* won the *Kenyon Review* Earthworks Indigenous Poetry Prize and a Western Heritage Award. Her books of essays include *Bury My Heart at Chuck E. Cheese's* (Washington State Book Award finalist), and *The Dreamcatcher in the Wry* (forthcoming). Midge is a columnist for *High Country News* and aspires to be the Distinguished Writer in Residence for Seattle's Space Needle.

Publications by Two Sylvias Press:

The Daily Poet: Day-By-Day Prompts For Your Writing Practice
by Kelli Russell Agodon and Martha Silano (Print and eBook)

The Daily Poet Companion Journal (Print)

Everything is Writable: 240 Poetry Prompts from Two Sylvias Press
by Kelli Russell Agodon and Annette Spaulding-Convy (Print)

Demystifying the Manuscript: Essays and Interviews on Creating a Book of Poems
edited by Susan Rich and Kelli Russell Agodon (Print)

Fire On Her Tongue: An Anthology of Contemporary Women's Poetry
edited by Kelli Russell Agodon and Annette Spaulding-Convy (Print and eBook)

The Poet Tarot and Guidebook: A Deck Of Creative Exploration (Print)

The Inspired Poet: Writing Exercises to Spark New Work
by Susan Landgraf (Print)

Horns, Winner of the 2022 Two Sylvias Press Wilder Prize
by Tiffany Midge (Print)

The Call of Paradise, Winner of the 2022 Two Sylvias Press Chapbook Prize
by Majda Gama (Print)

Omena Bay Testament, Winner of the 2021 Two Sylvias Press Wilder Prize
by Gail Griffin (Print)

At Night My Body Waits, Winner of the 2021 Two Sylvias Press Chapbook Prize
by Saúl Hernández (Print)

Nightmares & Miracles, Winner of the 2020 Two Sylvias Press Wilder Prize
by Michelle Bitting (Print)

Hallucinating a Homestead, Winner of the 2020 Two Sylvias Press
Chapbook Prize by Meg E. Griffitts (Print)

Shade of Blue Trees, Finalist 2019 Two Sylvias Press Wilder Prize
by Kelly Cressio-Moeller (Print)

Disappearing Queen, Winner of the 2019 Two Sylvias Press Wilder Prize
by Gail Martin (Print)

Deathbed Sext, Winner of the 2019 Two Sylvias Press Chapbook Prize
by Christopher Salerno (Print)

Crown of Wild, Winner of the 2018 Two Sylvias Press Wilder Prize
by Erica Bodwell (Print)

American Zero, Winner of the 2018 Two Sylvias Press Chapbook Prize
by Stella Wong (Print and eBook)

All Transparent Things Need Thundershirts, Winner of the 2017 Two Sylvias Press
Wilder Prize by Dana Roeser (Print and eBook)

Where The Horse Takes Wing: The Uncollected Poems of Madeline DeFrees
edited by Anne McDuffie (Print and eBook)

In The House Of My Father, Winner of the 2017 Two Sylvias Press Chapbook Prize
by Hiwot Adilow (Print and eBook)

Box, Winner of the 2017 Two Sylvias Press Poetry Prize
by Sue D. Burton (Print and eBook)

Tsigan: The Gypsy Poem (New Edition)
by Cecilia Woloch (Print and eBook)

PR For Poets
by Jeannine Hall Gailey (Print and eBook)

Appalachians Run Amok, Winner of the 2016 Two Sylvias Press Wilder Prize
by Adrian Blevins (Print and eBook)

Pass It On! by Gloria J. McEwen Burgess (Print)

Killing Marias
by Claudia Castro Luna (Print and eBook)

The Ego and the Empiricist, Finalist 2016 Two Sylvias Press Chapbook Prize
by Derek Mong (Print and eBook)

The Authenticity Experiment
by Kate Carroll de Gutes (Print and eBook)

Mytheria, Finalist 2015 Two Sylvias Press Wilder Prize
by Molly Tenenbaum (Print and eBook)

Arab in Newsland , Winner of the 2016 Two Sylvias Press Chapbook Prize
by Lena Khalaf Tuffaha (Print and eBook)

The Blue Black Wet of Wood, Winner of the 2015 Two Sylvias Press Wilder Prize
by Carmen R. Gillespie (Print and eBook)

Fire Girl: Essays on India, America, and the In-Between
by Sayantani Dasgupta (Print and eBook)

Blood Song
by Michael Schmeltzer (Print and eBook)

Community Chest
by Natalie Serber (Print)

Naming The No-Name Woman,
Winner of the 2015 Two Sylvias Press Chapbook Prize by Jasmine An (Print and
eBook)

Phantom Son: A Mother's Story of Surrender
by Sharon Estill Taylor (Print and eBook)

What The Truth Tastes Like
by Martha Silano (Print and eBook)

landscape/heartbreak
by Michelle Peñaloza (Print and eBook)

Earth, Winner of the 2014 Two Sylvias Press Chapbook Prize
by Cecilia Woloch (Print and eBook)

The Cardiologist's Daughter
by Natasha Kochicheril Moni (Print and eBook)

She Returns to the Floating World
by Jeannine Hall Gailey (Print and eBook)

Hourglass Museum
by Kelli Russell Agodon (eBook)

Cloud Pharmacy
by Susan Rich (eBook)

Dear Alzheimer's: A Caregiver's Diary & Poems
by Esther Altshul Helfgott (eBook)

Listening to Mozart: Poems of Alzheimer's
by Esther Altshul Helfgott (eBook)

The Wilder Series Poetry Book Prize

The Wilder Series Book Prize is an annual contest hosted by Two Sylvias Press. It is open to women over 50 years of age (established or emerging poets) and includes a $1000 prize, publication by Two Sylvias Press, 20 copies of the winning book, and a vintage, art nouveau pendant. Women submitting manuscripts may be poets with one or more previously published chapbooks/books or poets without any prior chapbook/book publications. The judges for the prize are Two Sylvias Press cofounders and coeditors, Kelli Russell Agodon and Annette Spaulding-Convy.

The Wilder Series Book Prize Winners and Finalists

2022: Tiffany Midge, *Horns* (Winner)

2021: Gail Griffin, *Omena Bay Testament* (Winner)

2020: Michelle Bitting, *Nightmares & Miracles* (Winner)

2019: Gail Martin, *Disappearing Queen* (Winner)
Kelly Cressio-Moeller, *Shade of Blue Trees* (Finalist)

2018: Erica Bodwell, *Crown of Wild* (Winner)

2017: Dana Roeser, *All Transparent Things Need Thundershirts* (Winner)

2016: Adrian Blevins, *Appalachians Run Amok* (Winner)

2015: Carmen R. Gillespie, *The Blue Black Wet of Wood* (Winner)
Molly Tenenbaum, *Mytheria* (Finalist)

www.ingramcontent.com/pod-product-compliance
Lightning Source LLC
Chambersburg PA
CBHW031140090426
42738CB00008B/1168